Tokyo

by Christina Leaf
Illustrated by Diego Vaisberg

BLASTOFF!
MISSIONS

BELLWETHER MEDIA
MINNEAPOLIS, MN

T0010024

Blastoff! Missions takes you on a learning adventure! Colorful illustrations and exciting narratives highlight cool facts about our world and beyond. Read the mission goals and follow the narrative to gain knowledge, build reading skills, and have fun!

Traditional Nonfiction

Narrative Nonfiction

Blastoff! Universe

MISSION GOALS

> FIND YOUR SIGHT WORDS IN THE BOOK.

> LEARN ABOUT IMPORTANT EVENTS IN TOKYO'S HISTORY.

> LEARN HOW TOKYO GREW INTO A MODERN CITY.

This edition first published in 2024 by Bellwether Media, Inc.

No part of this publication may be reproduced in whole or in part without written permission of the publisher. For information regarding permission, write to Bellwether Media, Inc., Attention: Permissions Department, 6012 Blue Circle Drive, Minnetonka, MN 55343.

Library of Congress Cataloging-in-Publication Data

Names: Leaf, Christina, author. | Vaisberg, Diego, illustrator.
Title: Tokyo / by Christina Leaf ; Diego Vaisberg [illustrator]
Description: Minneapolis, MN : Bellwether Media, 2024. | Series: Cities through time | Includes bibliographical references and index. | Audience: Ages 5-8 | Audience: Grades 2-3 | Summary: "Vibrant illustrations accompany information about the history of Tokyo. The narrative nonfiction text is intended for students in kindergarten through third grade." -- Provided by publisher.
Identifiers: LCCN 2023014282 (print) | LCCN 2023014283 (ebook) | ISBN 9798886873856 (library binding) | ISBN 9798886875232 (paperback) | ISBN 9798886875737 (ebook)
Subjects: LCSH: Tokyo (Japan)--History--Juvenile literature.
Classification: LCC DS896.62 .L43 2024 (print) | LCC DS896.62 (ebook) | DDC 952/.135--dc23/eng/20230328
LC record available at https://lccn.loc.gov/2023014282
LC ebook record available at https://lccn.loc.gov/2023014283

Text copyright © 2024 by Bellwether Media, Inc. BLASTOFF! MISSIONS and associated logos are trademarks and/or registered trademarks of Bellwether Media, Inc.

Editor: Betsy Rathburn   Designer: Andrea Schneider

Printed in the United States of America, North Mankato, MN.

This is **Blastoff Jimmy**! He is here to help you on your mission and share fun facts along the way!

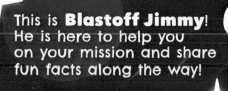

Table of Contents

Welcome to Tokyo! 4

On the Bay 6

A Modern City 12

The City Today 20

Glossary 22

To Learn More 23

Beyond the Mission 24

Index 24

Welcome to Tokyo!

Welcome to the biggest city in the world!

pre-1400s

Life is quiet here. Small villages sit along a bay. Fishermen pull catches from the water. **Buddhists** pray in a nearby **temple**.

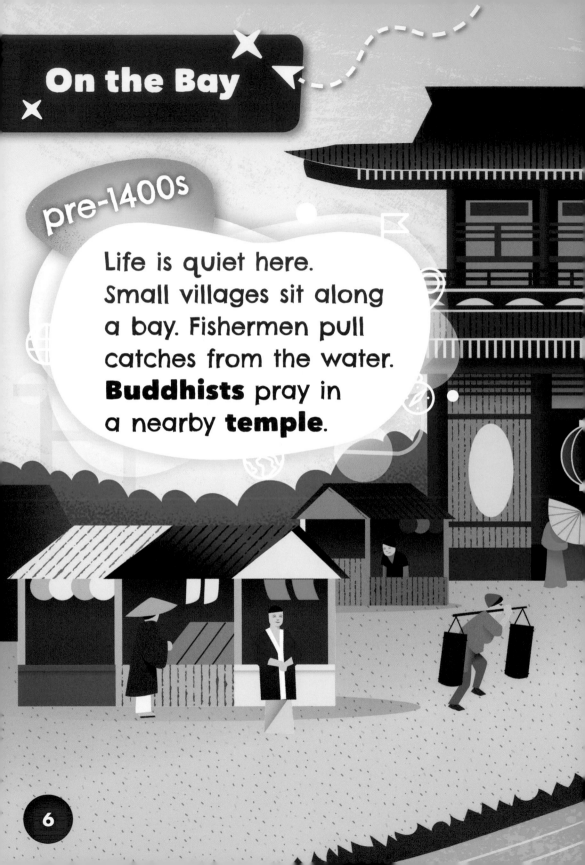

temple

Buddhist

Ōta Dōkan

▶JIMMY SAYS◀
Edo means "door to the bay" in Japanese.

8

1457

Warrior Ōta Dōkan looks over the land he won for his **lord**. The hill is easy to protect. The bay is good for trading. He will make Edo Castle on this spot!

1603

Tokugawa Ieyasu has taken control of Japan. He will rule as **shogun**. Edo Castle will be his home.

The castle is falling apart. But workers are already rebuilding. A new city will grow around it!

Edo Castle

emperor

1868

Japan's new **emperor** has moved to Edo Castle. He also renamed the city Tokyo. It means "eastern capital."

JIMMY SAYS

Japan was closed for more than 200 years. People could not leave. Traders could not enter.

More changes will come. Japan is looking to the world for new ideas and technology!

1914

Tokyo is changing quickly! Trains roll into the new **Western-style** Tokyo Station.

Tokyo Station

Men wear bowler hats while women wear long dresses. They stroll newly paved roads.

bowler hat

15

1945

Tokyo has seen one of the worst **raids** of World War II. U.S. planes bombed the city. Fires burned it to the ground. This deadly attack will quicken the end of the war.

1964

The rebuilt Tokyo is booming! Crowds have come to watch the **Olympic Games**. The new bullet train speeds people to the city.

monorail

bullet train

A **monorail** carries them around town. Tokyo is a modern city!

today

People hurry past wooden temples and steel skyscrapers. Gardens offer peaceful spots. Bright signs light up the night. **Tradition** and technology meet in Tokyo!

Tokyo Timeline

pre-1400s: Villages line the bay in the area that will be Tokyo

1457: Edo Castle is built

1603: Tokugawa Ieyasu becomes shogun and rebuilds Edo Castle

1868: Edo is renamed Tokyo

1914: Tokyo Station is completed

1945: Tokyo is bombed in World War II

1964: Tokyo hosts the Olympics and its bullet train is completed

Tokyo, Japan

Glossary

Buddhists–people who follow the teachings of Buddha

emperor–the ruler of an empire

lord–a high-ranking man who has power over others

monorail–a kind of train that travels on a track with a single rail

Olympic Games–worldwide summer or winter sports contests held in a different country every four years

raids–surprise attacks

shogun–a military leader who has political power

temple–a building used for worship

tradition–a custom, idea, or belief that has been handed down from one generation to the next

Western-style–in the style of countries in the western part of the world, especially Europe

To Learn More

AT THE LIBRARY

Claybourne, Anna. *Tokyo*. Oakland, Calif.: Lonely Planet, 2017.

Fehlen, Douglas J. *Explore Tokyo*. Mankato, Minn.: 12-Story Library, 2020.

Sabelko, Rebecca. *Japan*. Minneapolis, Minn.: Bellwether Media, 2023.

ON THE WEB

FACTSURFER

Factsurfer.com gives you a safe, fun way to find more information.

1. Go to www.factsurfer.com.

2. Enter "Tokyo" into the search box and click 🔍.

3. Select your book cover to see a list of related content.

BEYOND THE MISSION

> WHAT FACT FROM THE BOOK DID YOU THINK WAS THE MOST INTERESTING?

> WHICH POINT IN TOKYO'S HISTORY WOULD YOU LIKE TO VISIT?

> THINK ABOUT A CITY YOU HAVE VISITED. WHAT DO YOU THINK IT WAS LIKE IN THE PAST?

Index

bay, 6, 8, 9
Buddhists, 6, 7
Dōkan, Ōta, 8, 9
Edo Castle, 9, 10, 11, 12
emperor, 12
fishermen, 6
gardens, 20
Ieyasu, Tokugawa, 10
Japan, 5, 10, 13
monorail, 18, 19
name, 8, 12
Olympic Games, 18
people, 5, 13, 18, 20

roads, 15
shogun, 10
skyscrapers, 20
technology, 13, 20
temple, 6, 7, 20
timeline, 21
Tokyo Station, 14
traders, 9, 13
trains, 14, 18
villages, 6
World War II, 16